book *of* faith
Advent Reflections
You Shall Have a Song

Jeanette Bialas Strandjord
Paul E. Walters
Karoline M. Lewis
Philip Ruge-Jones
Debbie Trafton O'Neal

BOOK OF FAITH ADVENT REFLECTIONS
You Shall Have a Song

For information on the Book of Faith initiative and Book of Faith resources, go to www.bookoffaith.org.

 Book of Faith is an initiative of the
Evangelical Lutheran Church in America
God's work. Our hands.

Cover design: Running Design Group
Interior composition: PerfecType, Nashville, TN

ISBN 978-1-4514-2558-1

Manufactured in the U.S.A.

18   17   16   15   14   13   12   1   2   3   4   5   6   7   8   9   10

Contents

Introduction

"O sing to the LORD a new song; sing to the LORD, all the earth," Psalm 96:1 declares. This song of faith bubbles up from all living things in praise of God's amazing work of creating, renewing, and saving.

God promises, "You shall have a song" (Isaiah 30:29), even when things look the most bleak and hopeless. In a time like that, God provided a song about a servant who would bring justice and light to all the world. The lyrics of this song, recorded in Isaiah 42, are later echoed in the story of Jesus' life, death, and resurrection.

Mary, the mother of Jesus, sings with joy because of all the great things God has done and will do through her son. All who are lowly and powerless will be lifted up. The song's theme of justice sounds familiar, yet continually challenges us.

The apostle Paul sings in Philippians 2 about the mystery of a love that sets power aside to be with us. Christ Jesus did not cling to, clutch, or exploit the place of glory, but chose to come down to us and share our lot as human beings. More than that, he descended even further and willingly died on the cross. The song comes to a full crescendo as Paul tells us that nothing is more important than this one who made a "divine descent" so that we might have peace, salvation, and life.

Advent Reflections: You Shall Have a Song explores these four biblical songs, songs of God's justice and servant leadership. Hum along and learn the words of the songs as you move through the daily reflections, weekly Bible studies, and hands-on activities. Let the lyrics and notes of these songs take hold of you. Sing with gusto and share the songs with others so the chorus of faith and witness may grow. Let all the earth sing to the Lord!

Advent Reflections is a Book of Faith resource. In 2007 the Evangelical Lutheran Church in America (ELCA) reaffirmed the centrality of the Bible to

Christian life and faith, and at the same time recognized the reality of biblical illiteracy in the church. This resulted in the Book of Faith initiative, which invites us to open Scripture and join the conversation. By looking at the Bible through different lenses—historical, literary, Lutheran, and devotional—we can enter into a dialogue with God's Word in ways that lead to deeper understanding and spiritual growth. The emphasis in this book is on the devotional lens, but the other lenses are used to provide insights into Scripture as well. As a Book of Faith resource, *Advent Reflections* offers opportunities to open Scripture, look at it through different lenses, and join conversations with the Bible, with friends or family, with a small group, and, ultimately, with God.

How to Use This Book

Start this book on the first Sunday in Advent (four Sundays before Christmas), if possible. Put it in a prominent place in your home, purse, backpack, or briefcase so you'll be reminded to use it every day. Use the daily reflections, weekly Bible studies, and activities during the Advent season to explore and celebrate God's promise that *you* shall have a song.

Advent Reflections

This section guides you in a daily devotional time with a reflection, questions, and a prayer for every day in Advent (see pp. 13–69). Have a Bible handy each day so that you can read the text and then the reflection. Spend a few moments thinking about the "Questions to Ponder." Close your devotional time with the prayer, perhaps followed by a prayer of your own or a few moments of silence.

You can connect this devotional time with things that are already part of your daily routine. Here are a few suggestions for doing this. Ask others for their ideas as well. Read the Bible text, reflection, and prayer during a meal, coffee break, or bus ride. Consider the "Questions to Ponder" as you take a walk, wait in line, or spend some quiet time thinking and praying. When you are with friends and family members, talk about what you are reading and learning. Open your heart to four biblical songs about God's justice and servant leadership.

Bible Studies

Four Bible studies, one for each week in Advent, highlight the four main themes used in the daily reflections: God's New Song, Song of Light, Mary's Song, and Servant Song (see pp. 71–79). Use these Bible studies once a week on your own, with a friend or family member, in a small group that already exists, or in a new group formed with other people who are reading this book. If you are in a small group using the Bible studies in this book, be sure to take time for the daily reflections as well.

Activities

The Activities section (pp. 81–100) provides many hands-on ways for families with younger children to celebrate the Advent season. You may want to scan this entire section before Advent begins and pick out one or two activities for each week, or simply choose activities as the season goes along. Either way, focus on what is most doable and meaningful for your family, not on finishing every activity provided.

The Advent Blessings Wreath is an activity you can begin at the start of the season and build on each week. Hang this simple wreath in your home as a reminder of some of the wonderful ways God is blessing you and you are blessing others during this Advent season.

Our Writers

Week 1 Reflections and Bible Study: God's New Song

Jeanette Bialas Strandjord is a pastor at Williams Bay Lutheran Church in southeastern Wisconsin. Her work includes devotions, Bible studies, curriculum, and preaching resources. Preaching and teaching bring her great challenge and joy in her parish ministry. She lives with her husband, Jonathan, also a pastor, currently serving on the ELCA's churchwide staff.

Week 2 Reflections and Bible Study: Song of Light

Paul E. Walters serves as pastor of Lutheran Church of the Master, Troy, Michigan. He is coauthor of *Called by God to Serve* (Augsburg Fortress, 2004) and *Christ in Your Marriage* (Augsburg Fortress, 2007). He is a frequent contributor to sundaysandseasons.com. Paul enjoys writing stewardship plays filled with cowboy slang and pirate lingo. He and his wife, Brandy, are doing everything they can to keep up with their three amazing and energetic sons.

Week 3 Reflections and Bible Study: Mary's Song

Karoline M. Lewis is the Alvin N. Rogness Chair of Homiletics at Luther Seminary, St. Paul, Minnesota, and an ordained pastor. She has led conferences, workshops, and retreats throughout the United States and Canada and written several articles and books. She is a contributing writer for www.workingpreacher.org and cohost of the site's weekly podcast, *Sermon Brainwave*.

Week 4 Reflections and Bible Study: Servant Song

Philip Ruge-Jones is an associate professor of theology at Texas Lutheran University. His book *The Word of the Cross in a World of Glory* (Augsburg Fortress, 2008) offers an exploration of the way Christ's gift shapes our lives. He and his family learn biblical stories by heart and perform them. He is pleased to be a part of a welcoming community of compassion, Living Word Lutheran Church, in Buda, Texas.

Activities

Debbie Trafton O'Neal is an author, educator, and consultant who lives in the Seattle, Washington, area. She has written more than fifty books for children, families, and educators and has developed, written, and edited curriculum for more than twenty-five years. Creative, hands-on experiences are her favorite ways to teach and learn.

Advent Reflections

Week 1: God's New Song

Day 1: Sunday

Time to Sing!

Psalm 96

> *Key Verse:* O sing to the LORD a new song. Psalm 96:1

At the beginning of Advent, many of us take a long, deep breath and then dive in . . . into all those preparations and gatherings that are part of these four brief weeks that precede Christmas. Many of our activities are the same as last year: decorating, shopping, baking, visits with family and friends, children's Christmas program, and Christmas caroling. They are the same and yet not the same. This year we may not have some of our loved ones with us. They are gone, perhaps serving overseas in the military or gone to their heavenly home. This year we may not have the health and strength to build that snowman with the grandkids or to make that special Christmas bread everyone has come to expect and enjoy. Or this year we may have some new faces around the table as our family has grown. An entire year has passed since the last Advent season and we aren't, can't be, quite the same.

Whether it was a year of struggle and defeat or of plenty and victory, Psalm 96 called Israel to sing a new song. This open and joyous invitation was part of Israel's new-year celebration. God's people had come through one more year, and this new song celebrated the saving energy of God present and active in the new year and for all peoples of the earth. Nothing stays quite the same, and it is important for us to remember that God keeps up with the changes in us and in our world. God's love and power are new to us not only every year or every Advent but every minute of our lives.

On an annual caroling night not long ago, our church choir headed to the home of Sophie, a longtime member of the congregation who was dying of lung cancer. As we gathered around her bed, we sang. We sang all the old favorite carols she and her sister requested. Just when we thought it was probably time for us to go, Sophie said, "Oh, just one more, 'Jesus Loves Me.'" Sophie knew that her life was about to change in a way none of us had experienced firsthand. She needed, one more time, that good news of God's love in Jesus, to give her courage and peace in this new experience of dying. So we sang. We sang it twice, as she requested. We had a song to sing—God's song—and it brought courage and peace.

Questions to Ponder

- What has changed for you or your family in the last year? How or when have God's love and power been made new for you as you've experienced these changes?
- Who in your family, neighborhood, or worshiping community needs to hear God's song of saving grace this Advent? When and where will you sing it?

Prayer

Thank you, God, for your song of saving love, sung throughout the ages and most beautifully in Jesus Christ. Open our ears to hear your song anew every day, so we may live with courage and strength. Let your song be in our hearts and on our lips as we seek to serve you and our neighbor this Advent season. Amen.

Day 2: Monday

Listen and Tell!

Psalm 96

 Key Verse: Sing to the Lord, bless his name; tell of his salvation from day to day. Psalm 96:2

"Please let me know when you hear something," a good friend might say after you've just shared that you are awaiting the results of a lab test or confided that you had that final interview for a new job. Friends are eager to hear about what is happening in your life. They want you to tell them so that they may share in your news.

Psalm 96 is about telling good news. Several thousand years ago God's people, Israel, sang out the good news not only for themselves but for all the peoples of the world. They were busy telling that the Lord God is at work in their lives and in the whole world to set matters right. How good for us to turn off all our electronic devices, stop whatever we are doing, and sit quietly to listen to this faithful proclamation of God's saving work. Then, as we listen, we can learn the lyrics and hum the tune. Israel's ancient chorus sings the song to us and lives on in our singing too.

What do we do when we hear good news? We text, e-mail, twitter, or phone others. "I got the job!" or "It's a healthy baby boy!" is news just too good not to pass along. We have other news that is too good not to pass along, and there is a whole world waiting for this news. It is the good news that God is here at work in the baby Jesus born in Bethlehem—at work to set matters right. The salvation proclaimed in the psalms takes on flesh and blood in God's Son, Jesus. God has entered our ordinary lives so that grace and love become concrete. People who are poor and hungry need the good news that God is on their side. Gifts of food and care given in God's name bring this message. People who are depressed and despairing need to hear of God's love and power. God can lift them up through our words and actions. A materialistic world needs to hear that there is some-thing much more meaningful than what we buy and own. Tell the good news in the song you sing and in the help you give—this Advent and every day.

Questions to Ponder

- When do you take time to listen to the song of faith? Where and when could you set aside time to sit quietly, meditate, and pray? What psalm or song could you use?
- Sometimes a friend will greet you with "What's the good word?" How might you answer this question in light of Psalm 96:2-3? What might you do to help make the good news concrete in the lives of others? Where do matters need to be set right?

Prayer

Lord, help us make time and space to listen to the ancient song of good news. Help us let go of all demands, sit quietly, and listen to this good word of faith and praise. May listening then turn into singing, and our singing move us to share your love with others in words and concrete works of caring. Amen.

Day 3: Tuesday

Why Sing?

Psalm 96

Key Verse: . . . but the LORD made the heavens. Psalm 96:5b

"My cancer taught me a lot," Debbie said. She was only fifty-one years old when her doctor gave her the news. Now, a year later, and after she had come through months of painful chemotherapy and radiation, she had finally received a clean bill of health. The prognosis was excellent. During her time of treatment, she had been forced to think about the meaning of life and how she might face her own death. During the long ordeal, the psalms gave Debbie insight and sustained her spiritually. "I'm in the hands of the Creator," she would often say when I visited her in the hospital, "the one who made heaven and earth." Focusing on God as the creator of all things gave her peace and hope throughout her cancer treatment.

Debbie heard the ancient witness of God's people through the psalms, and it renewed her in body and spirit. Psalms gave her a song to sing in difficult times, a song of confidence. She trusted and was thankful for fine doctors, medical workers, and the support of family and friends. They embodied God's life-giving wisdom and power. But her absolute foundation and reason for confidence was God. God alone had created the heavens. God alone knows our coming and going. God alone keeps us in life and death. Debbie didn't compose these lyrics of good news; she received such words of confidence from God's people who had endured judgment, conflict, and exile and still continued to rely on God. In the face of their sin and the suffering inflicted by others, God's people trusted God to continue creating and making things new.

Debbie is now back singing in the church choir. Now more than ever she is committed to singing praise to God. This Advent she and the choir will sing of the God who comes close to us in Jesus, born so long ago in Bethlehem. They will praise God, who keeps creating life out of death. They will sing for the sheer joy of this good news, but they will also sing so others may hear this good news and receive hope.

Questions to Ponder

- Take a few minutes today to think about God and the meaning of life. Your life is in the hands of the Creator who acts to make all things new. What does this mean to you?
- Post today's Key Verse (or another Bible passage that renews your confidence in God's power and love) in a place where you will see it every day. How might you share this good news with others?

Prayer

O Lord, creator of heaven and earth, let me not forget that all things begin and end in you. May your powerful, creating love sustain me all my days so that I may face all life's challenges and suffering with confidence in your ever-present grace. May Israel's ancient song of trust and praise put the song of faith on my lips and in my heart. Amen.

Day 4: Wednesday

Sing in the Sanctuary

Psalm 96

🗨 *Key Verse:* . . . strength and beauty are in his sanctuary. Psalm 96:6b

Now Psalm 96 moves us into the sanctuary, God's holy place. Here the good news of the Lord's greatness is announced and experienced. The Lord has promised to be here with great power. God is no mere memory, and our worship in God's sanctuary is not just playacting. This is for real. As the community of ancient Israel gathered together, and as we gather together today in God's name, God's strength and beauty are present. God comes and we come. This is Advent living, for *advent* literally means "coming."

Lauren F. Winner, author of *Still: Notes on a Mid-faith Crisis* (HarperOne, 2012), found that the glow of her adult conversion to Christianity was fading. She writes that nothing seemed as certain as it once had, and she wasn't praying or believing anymore. Still, she found herself going to church and going back to church again and again. In an interview on National Public Radio's *All Things Considered* (February 25, 2012), she shared the memory of one of those Sundays when she did not want to go to church but did so anyway. During worship, a somewhat seedy woman sat down in the pew to the left of Winner and began tapping her finger against the wooden pew in front of her. Winner was irritated by the noise. Suddenly, without thinking about it, she found her left hand shooting out to cover the woman's hand and the tapping finger. Winner was horrified at what she had done, but the woman was not insulted. Instead, she gratefully took Winner's hand and held on to it. The two women continued to hold hands throughout the service. A potentially offensive action became a comfort to both the stranger and to Winner. "That is where I met Jesus that day," Winner said in the interview.

Worship of God and with one another in the sanctuary can sometimes seem outdated, boring, hypocritical, or meaningless. We forget that for all its imperfections, God promises to meet us in worship. God comes and we come, to be joined together with God and our neighbor. Ancient Israel teaches us that strength and beauty are in God's sanctuary. This is true for God's people of every time and place. As we gather in the Lord's sanctuary with fellow believers, God is there holding us close and holding us close to one another.

Questions to Ponder

- Do you remember a time when you did not want to go to church to worship? Why? If you went anyway, what happened?
- How or when do you experience God's strength and beauty in worship? How can you be a mirror of that for others?

Prayer

God of strength and beauty, draw us together in worship of you in your sanctuary. When we are tired or reluctant to pray or praise, put us in the pew anyway. When we gather, be present with us as we sing, pray, listen, and receive Holy Communion, so that we may receive your joy and blessing. Amen.

Day 5: Thursday

We Need to Sing Together

Psalm 96

 Key Verse: Ascribe to the LORD, O families of the peoples, ascribe to the LORD glory and strength. Psalm 96:7

In early March 2012 storms and tornadoes cut a destructive path through the Ohio and Tennessee River valleys, leaving whole communities in shambles and taking the lives of more than three dozen people. Hundreds of emergency workers, counselors, and clergy rushed to the communities to offer physical and spiritual help. They wisely advised survivors to come together. Coming together makes mutual sharing and support possible. News footage showed people gathering in circles of prayer and in churches for worship. Said one clergywoman interviewed on the Weather Channel: "We need to sing" at times like these. Singing connects us to one another and to God.

The writer of Psalm 96 knows the power of singing to God and encourages God's people to "ascribe to the LORD the glory due his name" (96:8a). It is not enough to gather in the sanctuary to receive God's strength and glory; God also calls us to respond. Our singing to the Lord is part of the conversation of faith. Singing helps faith live in the moment, even in the midst of disaster. Singing to the Lord helps us to get our bearings when we are disoriented, disheartened, and uncertain. The words of a hymn can enable us to express our lament, hope, and joy in ways we otherwise might not be able to do in daily conversation or in times of deep distress.

Singing to the Lord together, as Israel did so long ago, also gives us companions for the journey, whether we are singing praise and thanks or lament and petitions for help. The psalmist knows that we need one another and invites the "families of the peoples" to worship together. This is not an exclusive chorus requiring tryouts. Each and every voice is welcome, since God is creator of all. Individual voices then help support the singing of the whole song. When we feel uncertain about the melody or some part of the harmony, another's voice can steady and lead us. It works this way not only in actual singing but also in the support and care we give one another in the community of faith.

Questions to Ponder

- When do you sing with others? Think about a celebration or a disaster that brought your congregation or local community together to worship and pray. What did you all sing? What would you like to sing?
- When have you felt like singing with others? When has it been hard to join in the song of faith? Give thanks for those who have helped by singing next to you or supporting you with care and concern.

Prayer

Lord of glory and strength, gather us together in singing and worship this Advent season. May singing and worship help us to get our bearings in a season that can be disorienting and stressful. Help us to invite others into this faithful chorus so that our sung prayer and praise may strengthen us and draw us closer to one another. Give us ears to listen for those who struggle with singing, so we may give support and encouragement. Amen.

Day 6: Friday

Now Appearing Live

Psalm 96

Key Verse: Say among the nations, "The LORD is king!" Psalm 96:10a

Are you ready for Christmas? Have that Christmas Eve menu planned? Is all the decorating done? As we anticipate the celebration of Christ's birth, we can certainly feel some pressure to get ready and to create that perfect Christmas, whether we are trying to duplicate Christmases past or to copy idealistic portrayals of Christmas celebrations by the entertainment and commercial industries. We may also get caught up in comparing ourselves to others: Do I decorate as well as my brother-in-law, who last year had a Santa and sleigh on top of his house? Worry grows as we start to feel it's up to us to create the best Christmas ever. But it is not.

We do not create Christmas; we share it. The good news of God's presence and grace comes to us. This is just what the writer of Psalm 96 is saying in verse 10: "Say . . . , 'The LORD is king!'" God is here! God rules! This is a live appearance! Just announcing this good news brings it to life for all the nations and for us. God's people Israel knew this. That's why their songs or psalms tell us to declare, ascribe, worship, and say. God's presence and power are for real, so say it right here and right now. The writer of Hebrews puts it this way: "The word of God is living and active" (4:12). We do not create the word of good news; we receive it. Then we announce it so others may receive it too.

Some years ago a family close to ours had very little money for Christmas presents. They did not make any appeal for help but decided to draw names so each person would receive one homemade gift on Christmas Eve. When they put up their Christmas tree, they placed their entire manger scene under it, and nothing else. On Christmas Eve they attended the candlelight service at church, came home to a modest meal, read the Christmas story, and then each family member, in turn, opened a single gift. After that they shared Christmas memories and sang carols. Years later the two children still remember that Christmas as one of their happiest and most peaceful. It had been so simple—focused on God's gift of Jesus. All that other stuff wasn't necessary.

When Martha was worried and distracted, Jesus told her, "There is need of only one thing" (Luke 10:42). Good words for Advent. This Advent, don't allow worry and anxiety to overwhelm you and your family. Focus on what God has done, is doing, and will do. In Jesus Christ, God is here and God reigns!

Questions to Ponder

- You do not create Christmas but share it. How does hearing this help you?
- How might you focus on God's rule and God's gift of Jesus this Christmas? Think about ways you might simplify your gift giving and celebrating in order to help keep Jesus as the reason for the season.

Prayer

O Lord, you are King! Help me to focus on you this Advent season and keep the good news of the birth of Jesus your Son as the heart and center of my preparation and celebration. Amen.

Day 7: Saturday

A Global Chorus
Psalm 96

> 🔖 *Key Verse:* Then shall all the trees of the forest sing for joy before the LORD; for he is coming . . . to judge the earth. Psalm 12b-13a

Some summers ago I visited the Lutheran Theological Seminary (LTS) in Hong Kong and worshiped with other visitors there. Hong Kong is a city with more than seven million people of various ethnic and cultural backgrounds, so it is not uncommon to find people representing twenty or more different nationalities at LTS. One warm evening people gathered there from places such as Norway, England, France, mainland China, various parts of the United States, Australia, Malaysia, and India. It was a Psalm 96 experience.

We worshiped, singing songs and tunes from one another's cultures and often using our own languages in confession and prayer. The two most common words spoken in unison, emerging out of the cacophony of our separate languages, were "Jesus Christ." It was an enriching and expanding experience to share worship and faith with such a diverse group of God's people. With all of our differences, God had gathered us, and together we named God as creator and Jesus Christ as Lord. We were a global chorus. God connected us and held us, lifting us beyond our individual selves and communities in order to praise and serve God. Worshiping in a simple chapel at the top of the lush green mountain, To Fung Shan, and gazing out at the forested mountains around us, it seemed that "all the trees of the forest" were singing too.

Psalm 96 sings of a God who rules not only Israel but all of creation. God comes to judge the earth with righteousness and truth. This is good news because it means God comes and continues to come year in and year out to set matters right. God intervenes in our lives and our world to bring God's mercy and justice into places and situations where there is inequality, oppression, and destruction. God seeks to break down the barriers that divide us and to unite us in something much larger than our own backgrounds or identities—faith in God.

In Advent we celebrate the birth of Christ and also the hope of Christ's appearing again. That hope is good news, because then God's rule will be perfect and there will be righteousness and truth in all of God's creation. Until that day comes we can still sing of God's presence, mercy, and justice in our world now. And we do not sing alone. We are part of the global chorus of peoples around the world.

Questions to Ponder

- Reflect on a "Psalm 96 experience" you have had. How did the voices or efforts of many different people come together in a new or unexpected way to praise and serve God?
- Where in your personal relationships, congregation, community, or world do you see God working for mercy and justice in the midst of disagreement, conflict, or disaster?

Prayer

Draw us into your global chorus, O Lord, that we may receive a vision of the unity, justice, and joy you desire for us and all the earth. May we live and sing as people of hope, trusting that you rule faithfully now and forever. Amen.

Week 2: Song of Light

Day 8: Sunday

A Holy Servant

Isaiah 42:1-9

Key Verse: Here is my servant, whom I uphold,
　　my chosen, in whom my soul delights;
　I have put my spirit upon him;
　　he will bring forth justice to the nations. Isaiah 42:1

Wouldn't it be wonderful if God would fix all our problems and make difficulties disappear in an instant? God would take away our pain, give us an infusion of cash that would wipe away our debt, and make that difficult coworker or neighbor or relative behave better.

God, however, is not a divine ATM machine, dispensing whatever we want whenever we ask. And despite the claims of some, God never promises to fix our lives and make everything easy for us. Instead God promises to walk with us in our journey and give us what we need to face what each day brings. God sends a holy servant into our lives and into the world to bring justice to the nations.

Who is this holy servant? There are two schools of thought on this. One idea is that the servant Isaiah refers to is a specific person who will come and do all these wonderful things. Another idea is the servant is not one person but all of Israel, so all of God's people are responsible for bringing these wonderful things to pass.

Then there is a third possibility: that the text refers to an individual and to all of God's people, both at the same time. Even as we might see these words pointing toward Jesus, they are also a reminder that we are all responsible to hear the good news of the gospel and respond. So we pray faithfully, asking for the maturity to be responsible with the money God has blessed us with. We pray for the patience, wisdom, and grace to deal with difficult people. We pray for the courage to be numbered among those who bring justice into the world.

Through it all we *wait* in these Advent days. We await the celebration of the birth of Jesus yet again. But even more we wait for the fullness of God's kingdom. We wait for justice and mercy to prevail. We wait for the day when we know for certain that Jesus walks with us through everything each day brings. We wait with longing for the day we can sing with joy, "Arise, your light has come!" (ELW 314).

Questions to Ponder

- What are you waiting for God to fix in your life? What do you need from God to grow through this challenge?
- How are you called to bring justice to the world?

Prayer

Lord of light and song of my heart, open my eyes to see your many blessings. Strengthen me for serving even as I wait for the glory of your kingdom. Amen.

Day 9: Monday

The Promise of Justice

Isaiah 42:1-9

> *Key Verse:* He will not cry or lift up his voice,
>   or make it heard in the street;
>   a bruised reed he will not break,
>   and a dimly burning wick he will not quench;
>   he will faithfully bring forth justice. Isaiah 42:2-3

Welcome to Monday, the beginning of the workweek and the return to weekday routines. Even if you are retired, the rhythm and feel of Monday through Friday are different from Saturday and Sunday. Monday is the day you discover what the week will bring. It is the day the news cycle starts afresh.

Some weeks it is the day when good news starts coming, the sort of news that brings a smile to your face. Then there are those other weeks. You know the ones—when Monday brings enough challenges for the whole week and you almost dread what you will face on Tuesday. These are the weeks you sit alone somewhere and clench your hands into fists, shaking with anger, frustration, and more. Or you look at the days ahead with dread and fear.

Yet we read that the servant "will not cry or lift up his voice." Even with all the injustices in the world, even with all the struggles and difficulties, the servant manages to find a way to take it all on and move forward in faith. Who doesn't want to be like that? We want to be able to take on everything and move forward with confidence. We want that, but reality comes crashing in on all of us eventually.

In spite of all of this, Advent, a season of hope and preparation, promise and possibility, comes to us anew each year with the holy promise of God's presence with us through all we face. This is the holy, calming presence of grace, the promise we rediscover in a kind word from a stranger, or a surprise phone call or e-mail from a forgotten friend. Time and again we encounter the promise that we do not walk alone. The promise is ours forever: whatever comes, God, in Christ, is with us.

Still, from God there is more; there is always more. There is also the promise of a coming justice, of mercy continuing to unfold in, with, and under our lives. So we hope and trust in the promise of the glorious day when suffering is no more, when tears are dried forever, and when the kingdom of God comes into this world in its fullness.

You can hear these Advent promises as you sing the hope-filled hymn "Comfort, Comfort Now My People" (ELW 256):

> "Comfort, comfort now my people; tell of peace!" So says our God.
> Comfort those who sit in darkness mourning under sorrow's load.
> To God's people now proclaim that God's pardon waits for them!
> Tell them that their war is over; God will reign in peace forever.

Questions to Ponder

- How do you find comfort when you are facing difficulties?
- When have you been surprised by a chance reminder of grace?

Prayer

God of comfort and peace, be with me this day and every day. Send your messengers into my life to remind me of your presence and promises and fill me with hope. Amen.

Day 10: Tuesday

Our Light in the Darkness

Luke 1:67–79

Key Verse: "By the tender mercy of our God,
the dawn from on high will break upon us,
to give light to those who sit in darkness and in the shadow of death,
to guide our feet into the way of peace." Luke 1:78-79

It was an ordinary Sunday morning. Several people were standing just inside the front door of the church when a young man walked in. The word *Hope* was stitched in white letters on the front of his navy blue winter hat. This led to several jokes about how wonderful it was that Hope just walked into the church! Then the man explained he was a graduate of Hope College in Holland, Michigan.

Wouldn't it be wonderful if hope could just walk right into our lives? Hope: that optimistic, trusting view of the future. Hope: that confidence in the days to come. Hope, which too often seems nothing more than an elusive and too often empty promise.

Hope, but a different sort of hope than the world points to, is what Advent is all about. Our Advent hope, our Christian hope, is not grounded in outrageous promises. Our Christian hope is grounded in the reality of the cross. Our hope grows from our knowledge that God has acted in amazing ways in the lives of people since the dawn of time. Our hope is grounded in the powerful reality that even now we know there are beautiful ways God is acting in the lives of people each and every day. Trusting in the past, celebrating the present, we can look to the future with hope-filled confidence. If God has acted once, surely God will act again and again.

So we wait and watch and prepare. We turn our eyes to the cross, watching the glorious light of Jesus rising in our lives. You see this light breaking in through the slats of blinds drawn across hospital room windows. You see the light streaming through stained glass church windows, in the brightness of the sun reflecting off newly fallen snow, and in a child's smile that lights up a room.

You see this light shining in the darkness wherever you see the promise of God's mercy and compassion alive and active in the world.

Still, we long for more, fully knowing God's kingdom is always just beyond our human abilities. So we pray, not that the world would suddenly become perfect, but that God would be active in our lives. What a beautiful prayer from Luke's Gospel: Guide our feet into the way of peace. Peace is a journey, not a destination. The way of peace is the path we travel in this life. These Advent days, may our feet find paths of peace and may hope light the darkness, as we sing of God's mercy that will "drive away the gloom of death and lead us into peace" (ELW 250, stanza 3).

Questions to Ponder

- Where do you see the light of God's kingdom shining in the world?
- When have you noticed God guiding your feet into the way of peace?

Prayer

Open my eyes, merciful God, that I may see the glory of your kingdom shining in the darkness of this world. Lead me each day to bring messages of peace to those in need. Amen.

Day 11: Wednesday

Praying Constantly

Philippians 1:3-11

Key Verse: I thank my God every time I remember you, constantly praying with joy in every one of my prayers for all of you, because of your sharing in the gospel from the first day until now.
Philippians 1:3-5

There are two basic styles of knitting: English and Continental. The results look the same, but it takes about twice as long to knit in the English style, due to the extra motions involved.

It is not just with knitting that we make things more complicated and more difficult than they need to be. Consider prayer. A disciple said to Jesus, "Lord, teach us to pray" (Luke 11:1). So Jesus taught the disciples the Lord's Prayer. From this one prayer, we may sometimes get the impression that all prayers must have a similar form and grace. Or we worry that prayers should use formal language and poetic turns of phrase. Maybe you think that to pray properly you should sit at a certain table with a candle lit, a Bible open before you, and speak the perfect words clearly and carefully.

Advent is a season that invites a return to prayer, but prayer does not have to be formal or restricted. Prayers can be elegant and poetic, to be sure, but simple and even raw, demanding prayers are heard by God as well. In his letter to the church in Philippi, Paul tells the people he prays for them every time he remembers them. Your prayers can be as immediate and as simple. How many times during the day does a thought or memory of someone you know and love pass through your mind? Prayer does not need a perfect location or flowery speech. Faithful prayers can be as simple as, "Jesus, take care of my friend Juan."

Fill these Advent days with prayer. See how often you can pray each day. How often are you moved to lift up a word of thanksgiving for someone in your life? How often are you moved by a name or a news story or an e-mail to ask God to help someone in some way? How can you fill your days with prayer?

Your prayer could be as simple as recalling the beloved Advent hymn "O Come, O Come, Emmanuel" (ELW 257). How wonderful to mark the season by praying these words:

> O come, O come, Emmanuel,
> and ransom captive Israel,
> that mourns in lonely exile here
> until the Son of God appear.
> Rejoice! Rejoice!
> Emmanuel shall come to you, O Israel.

Questions to Ponder

- What are some obstacles to your prayer life?
- What moves you to pray?

Prayer

Open my mouth, O Lord, and may my lips declare your praise. May your Holy Spirit lead me to pray constantly, giving thanks, seeking guidance, and pleading for help and grace for all who are in need. Amen.

Day 12: Thursday

Celebrating Creation

Isaiah 42:1-9; Genesis 1:1—2:4

Key Verse: Thus says God, the LORD,
who created the heavens and stretched them out,
who spread out the earth and what comes from it,
who gives breath to the people upon it
and spirit to those who walk in it. Isaiah 42:5

On the night of a new moon, the moon is full but lies directly between the sun and the earth so it cannot be seen by the naked eye. Each night between a new moon and the next full moon, the night sky grows brighter.

As this Advent journey continues, consider stepping outside each night, if only for a few minutes. Is the moon dark, full, or in between? Notice the brightness of the stars during a new moon. Look for sharper shadows as the moon brightens. If the nights are cold where you live, let your skin experience the sensation. Feel alive in the crispness of the night air. Even these small actions can help connect you to the wonder and glory of God's creation.

All this is a gift from God. None of these things just happened. Everything has been brought into being and continues to be sustained by the gracious power of God. In these Advent days it is good to remember that the renewal God promises is not just the renewal of each person's life, but the renewal of all creation. The amazing promise from Revelation, "Then I saw a new heaven and a new earth" (21:1a), is a promise that Jesus comes to redeem not just people, but everything in all of creation that is broken.

God has entrusted humanity with the responsibility to care for creation. Recycling is not just a responsible thing to do; it is also a faithful action. Recycling is faithful because it helps reduce the need for landfills, and the need to harvest even more from the natural world. Recycling cares for God's good creation. The same could be said for insulating your home, walking rather than driving, and many other activities that preserve and protect the earth.

So step out into the crisp darkness on this night. If snow happens to be falling, lift up your face and feel the cold flakes brush your cheeks. If the night is clear, notice the stars. All this is a gift from God, the "Creator of the stars of night" (ELW 245).

Questions to Ponder

- What are some choices you have made to protect and preserve the gift of creation?
- What is your favorite place in this world?

Prayer

God of creation, open my eyes to the wonder of your world. Open my heart to care for the world you have made, as I prepare to celebrate the coming Savior. Amen.

Day 13: Friday

Preparing the Way

Luke 3:1-20

> 🗨 *Key Verse:* The word of God came to John son of Zechariah in the wilderness. He went into all the region around the Jordan, proclaiming a baptism of repentance for the forgiveness of sins. Luke 3:2b-3

God has given us the gift of four Gospels, each telling the story of Jesus. Each Gospel tells the story of Jesus—his life, teaching, healing, suffering, death, and resurrection. While the Gospels agree on the outline of the story, they differ in the details. It is interesting to consider what can be left out of the story of Jesus. You might be surprised. You don't need the parables of the good Samaritan or the prodigal son. Only Luke includes those. You do not need a Christmas story. Without Luke we would not have baby Jesus in a manger, or the shepherds. Without Matthew there would be no wise men. John never gives Mary, the mother of Jesus, a name. Yet without John there is no wedding in Cana of Galilee, no turning water into wine. The Lord's Prayer only appears in Matthew and Luke.

Jesus heals in all the Gospels. He teaches in all the Gospels. The cross, the passion, the suffering and dying and rising of Jesus are certainly in all the Gospels. And John the Baptist appears in all four Gospels. It would seem you cannot tell the story of Jesus without John the Baptist. We need John the Baptist crying out in the wilderness, calling to the people, "Prepare the way of the Lord."

With so many things that grab our attention and distract us from Jesus, we need John and others like him to point us to Jesus. We need to be reminded of the gift of the cross and the hope we find there.

This is not always a Jesus we want to look at. Infant Jesus needing us to take care of him is often easier to deal with. A Jesus who leaves us to our own devices, pats us on the back, and tells us we are good and fine people is a Jesus we like to have around. Not the Jesus on the cross.

It is so easy, especially at this time of year, to run all over town, trying to get the perfect gift, trying to prepare the perfect meal, trying to make the holidays be just like you want them to be. In the middle of all that chaos, we need John the

Baptist reminding us that the reason for the season is Jesus. It is his birth, his coming into the world that we are celebrating.

Like John the Baptist, we are called to point to Jesus. At some time in your life, someone loved you and loved Jesus enough to point you to Jesus. As faithful followers of Jesus, we are called to return the favor. This does not have to mean knocking on doors and talking to strangers. Start at home. Tell your spouse, your significant other, your children, grandchildren, nieces, nephews, aunts, and uncles. Tell those people who love you and trust you. Tell them how your life is changed for the better by the presence of Jesus. Let John's message become your message:

> On Jordan's bank the Baptist's cry
> announces that the Lord is nigh;
> awake and hearken, for he brings
> glad tidings of the King of kings!
> ("On Jordan's Bank the Baptist's Cry," ELW 249, stanza 1)

Questions to Ponder

- What must be included to tell the story of Jesus?
- When have you played the role of John the Baptist, pointing others to Jesus?

Prayer

Gracious God, you sent John the Baptist to point the way and lead many to faith. Use me according to your will to share the faith that is in me and give glory to your holy name. Amen.

Day 14: Saturday

Ready for Us Already

Luke 24:1-12; Isaiah 42:1-9

 Key Verse: See, the former things have come to pass,
and new things I now declare;
before they spring forth,
I tell you of them. Isaiah 42:9

This is grace plain and simple: Jesus acts before we need it, knowing what we will need. We need Jesus to die and rise so the promise of new, resurrected life will be ours. Jesus did this before we were even born, knowing we would be captive to sin and unable to free ourselves.

This is the way God functions. We trust in the future because God has already acted in our lives and in the world to guarantee our final future. Because the ultimate outcome of our lives is not in doubt, we can live faithfully and boldly. We can risk failure, trusting all the while in the one who promises to walk with us through whatever comes our way.

So on those days when it feels like you are swinging from a trapeze high above the earth, without a net, do not fear. God has already prepared your future. God has plans that even now are unfolding into a beautiful and amazing future. Trust that God is your net, even when life gets scary and dangerous. Trust in God to sustain you when you are exhausted and frustrated.

As you make your Advent plans and preparations, do the shopping, wrap the presents, plan the holiday meals, and find those thoughtful and heartfelt gifts for the people you love, look for opportunities to be bold and daring in your faith. Listen for the still, small voice of God calling to you out of the hustle and bustle of holiday crowds. Is there a neighbor who does not have family nearby? You could invite that person to share a Christmas meal with you. Is there someone who has recently moved into the neighborhood? A plate of cookies is a wonderful way to start a friendship.

Could God be calling you to something more? It is a hurting world in so many ways, and the holiday season can be particularly difficult for many people. How can you offer comfort, support, and a sign of grace for someone in need? During these Advent days as you prepare your home, take time to prepare your heart as well, so you can sing with joy and passion, "All earth is hopeful" (ELW 266).

Questions to Ponder

- How do God's past actions change your life this day?
- How can you share God's grace and love with someone this very day? Can you write a letter, send an e-mail or text message, make a phone call?

Prayer

Gracious God, you have forgiven me before I even knew I needed it. You have redeemed me from before my birth. Grant me faith to share words of hope with the people I meet this day. Amen.

Week 3: Mary's Song

Day 15: Sunday

Cause for Joy

Luke 1:46-55

> *Key Verse:* And Mary said, "My soul magnifies the Lord, and my spirit rejoices in God my Savior." Luke 1:46-47

Ironically, during the season of Advent, amid all of the preparations for Christmas, it can be hard to find and feel joy. Perhaps we expect joy to come to us or imagine that it should be automatic this time of year. Maybe we equate joy with happiness or a *laissez-faire* attitude toward life. Or we believe it is simply a mind-set—"just choose joy," to paraphrase a popular advertising slogan.

As a young woman living in the ancient town of Nazareth, Mary has little cause for joy. She knows her place. She is fully aware of her situation. Life in that time was difficult, and most people were barely able to get by. How would she and Joseph provide for a baby? How would they raise this child? How would people recognize him as the Son of God? Under the circumstances, Mary could easily be filled with worry and fear. And yet she sings a song filled with joy: "My soul magnifies the Lord, and my spirit rejoices in God my Savior."

How can Mary sing at a time like this? What is it about her or in her that she can muster this kind of praise for God and for life? It's easy to think of Mary as someone extraordinary, someone we could never be like. But keep in mind that she is a very ordinary person from a very ordinary place. The first words of her song clue us in to what is happening.

While we have a tendency to look at salvation as just one moment in time or a far-off afterlife, a resurrection security, a heavenly IRA, or a future reward for a life well lived, Mary sees salvation as right here and right now. God is her Savior, and this God is acting in her life and in the world to bring mercy and justice. This God has saved her, chosen her, and rejoices in her.

Mary sings for joy at what God has done, is doing, and will do. Mary's song is our song because God our Savior brings joy to ordinary people, wherever we are, even amid the challenges, frustrations, and difficulties of life.

Questions to Ponder

- What gives you joy? When and where and with whom do you experience true joy?
- What does it mean for you to call God your Savior? How do you define salvation?

Prayer

God of joy, as we await your presence among us, help us see that your saving acts are all around us. Help us recognize your salvation in your constant love and joy in our lives. Amen.

Day 16: Monday

To Be Favored

Luke 1:46-55

> *Key Verse:* "... for he has looked with favor on the lowliness of his servant. Surely, from now on all generations will call me blessed." Luke 1:48

To be looked upon with favor is a big deal. For various reasons, as a Lutheran girl and preacher's kid, I ended up in a Catholic high school. I remember being surprised and amazed when I first attended an Annunciation Day mass at San Domenico School for Girls. Amid unfamiliar ritual, I had some sense that this was not an event or day acknowledged or celebrated by Lutherans. But the main thing I remember is being surrounded by girls, by my friends, and thinking, God has looked with favor on us. God has regarded me.

In the story of the annunciation or announcement to Mary (Luke 1:26-38), an angel named Gabriel comes to her and says, "Greetings, favored one! The Lord is with you." Mary's initial response is worth significant pause: she is perplexed. She is at a loss for words, completely bewildered by the possibility that God regards or notices her. (Me? Who am I? Why am I favored? How can the Lord be with me?) Gabriel then tells Mary the big news that she's going to be pregnant with a son, but not just any son, the "Son of the Most High," no less, from David's family line, with a never-to-end kingdom. (Okay, what? This should not be happening.) Mary finally finds the words to ask, "How can this be?"

Mary's utter surprise in this encounter with Gabriel is no obligatory, automatic, obedient response. It is part of her incredible journey of faith in God. It is a prelude to her song in Luke 1:46-55. Her astonishment gives way to recognizing and acknowledging God's favor and regard for her. The prelude helps us hear Mary's song for what it truly is—an extraordinary and profound witness to what happens when God is active in our lives.

In this season of Advent, in the midst of everything that is the season for you (fill in the blanks here), what would it be like to experience, to know, that God favors you? This is no small thing, especially when we realize we don't deserve

God's favor and regard. Mary's song can help us see that so much of our sense of identity is based on expectations, so much of what we call dedication is only obedience, and so much of our sense of worthiness lies in the opinions of others. We construct our identities on the basis of what is expected of us. We do what we do to please others. We define ourselves through the lens of another, believing that our worth can be decided by those who think they know us. How much we need to hear these words with Mary: we are blessed. God sees us and knows us and loves us—where we are and for who we are.

Questions to Ponder

- Think about a time you felt like you were lifted up from a place of lowliness, like God brought you back from the brink . . . to yourself, or were called back from a place that was not fully you. What do you remember most from that experience?
- John O'Donohue writes, "One of the deepest longings of the human soul is to be seen." When have you been seen for who you truly are? What was that like?

Prayer

God of grace, because you became one of us, you have committed yourself to all the complexities of what it means to be human. Be with us as we work our way through the challenges and joys of our humanity. May we hear in Mary's song your regard and favor for us too. Amen.

Day 17: Tuesday

The Mighty Acts of God

Luke 1:46-55

Key Verse: "For the Mighty One has done great things for me, and holy is his name." Luke 1:49

"The Mighty One has done great things for me." These words are not mere lip service for Mary. Her song is possible only because of what God has done for her and for her cousin Elizabeth. God has saved Mary, noticed her, favored her, and intervened in her life and in the world. Elizabeth and her husband, Zechariah, had endured the pain of infertility, and not only that—in their day a childless woman was seen as a disgrace. They had grown old, with no more hope of children, when an angel appeared to Zechariah and announced that they would have a son, John. (He would later become known as John the Baptist.) After she becomes pregnant, Elizabeth says, "This is what the Lord has done for me when he looked favorably on me and took away the disgrace I have endured among my people" (Luke 1:25).

Mary sings about mighty acts of God that once seemed impossible: God's regard for Mary, God's work in Elizabeth's life, and God's choice to become human. The angel Gabriel's declaration that "nothing will be impossible with God" (1:37) finds its deepest meaning in the unfolding of these impossibilities. A barren, elderly woman is pregnant. A young teenage girl from a nothing town is favored and will give birth to the Son of the Most High. Even the impossible is possible.

One of the high points in Mary's song is when we sense, when we realize, that she has moved from seeing the impossible to seeing the possible. In that movement, she is able to express and give voice to God's activity in her life. Mary helps us see that God's possibility can ring new and true and whole in the midst of a world, our world, and our lives that know only impossibility. For Mary and for us today, to say God "has done great things for me" means embracing, realizing, and imagining the impossible possibility of God.

Questions to Ponder

- What in your life or in the world could God's possibility turn around?
- Name some of the great things God has done in your life. What makes them great?

Prayer

God of possibility, in this season of Advent sometimes we forget that the most impossible thing happened, that you became flesh, one of us. Help us remember that nothing is impossible for you. Amen.

Day 18: Wednesday

Genes Matter

Luke 1:46-55

> *Key Verse:* "His mercy is for those who fear him from generation to generation." Luke 1:50

There is something powerful and poignant about Luke 1:50, as simple as it appears to be. From generation to generation God has shown mercy, and now Mary receives that mercy. She sees herself in God's history. This is a powerful acknowledgment of God's active love, manifested throughout history. God has been merciful to generations of God's people, and Mary realizes she is now in that line, part of this heritage.

This is an extraordinary statement. Here's Mary, an unmarried, pregnant teenager from the wrong side of the tracks. Yet she now finds herself related to the likes of Sarah, Abraham, Moses, Rachel, David, and Ruth, to name only a few of our ancestors in the Bible. In the Gospel of Luke, Jesus' lineage traces all the way back to Adam and Eve, the first human beings. Matthew's Gospel follows this family tree back to Abraham and Sarah, and John tells us Jesus was present from the very beginning, before the world was created. The differences between the Gospels with regard to Jesus' lineage give us clues to understanding the identity of Jesus, the meaning of Jesus, and the portrait of Jesus for each Gospel writer. Luke's tracing of Jesus' origins and family tree through all the generations back to Adam and Eve is much more than a genealogical, historical statement of fact or observation. That Jesus stands in the line of Adam reiterates the ordinariness and commonality of Jesus' presence in the world. Jesus here is for everyone, including people who are outcast and marginalized and those we might immediately set aside as unworthy of Jesus' ministry or God's salvation. The first people to witness Jesus' entry in the world are not the wise men from the East, but the lowly shepherds. Mary, an everyday, common woman, understands that her lineage connects to the first humans, to Eve and to Adam. Like them, she is made in the image of God.

We too find ourselves as part of this family tree. In our family of origin we may have been told we are unworthy by family members over the years. Maybe we have based our worth on who is in our family tree. Maybe we are embarrassed about certain relatives or where we have come from. Whatever our circumstances, Mary's song reminds us that God's mercy is for ordinary, everyday people. Jesus was born in a stable, amid the animals and the straw, and rested in a manger. We belong to his family, the family of God.

Questions to Ponder

- What traits, stories, or heirlooms have been passed down from generation to generation in your family?
- How is the family of God different from your own family of origin? What difference does that make?

Prayer

God of promise, you have brought us into your family, and that puts us in some amazing company. In Advent times of family and fellowship, may we see in these moments a glimpse of your love for us. Amen.

Day 19: Thursday

Lifted Up

Luke 1:46-55

> *Key Verse:* "He has shown strength with his arm; he has scattered the proud in the thoughts of their hearts. He has brought down the powerful from their thrones, and lifted up the lowly." Luke 1:51-52

Mary's story shows a transformation from "How can this be?" (1:34) to "Here am I; . . . let it be with me according to your word" (1:38). We would do well to imagine that not everything is settled for her when she says, "Here I am." It is no small journey for her to go from peasant girl to prophet, from Mary to mother of God, from denial to discipleship. Few of us can claim this kind of radical transformation, but in a very real way, this is the appropriate transition from Advent to Christmas. Mary's story moves us all from who we think we are to who God has called us to be, from observant believer to confessing apostle. Remarkably, impossibly, Mary's story also demands that we recognize the very transformation of God. It is no small journey to go from our comfortable perceptions of God to seeing God in the manger, vulnerable, helpless, and dependent. Yet this is the promise of Christmas.

Mary's song proclaims God's ability to transform things, turning things upside down, providing strength and justice, undercutting the proud, and pulling the powerful from their thrones. The problem with power is not that power itself is bad, but that it is often wielded from a place of privilege, separation, and hierarchy rather than mercy, unity, and mutual respect. Those who are powerful often prefer thrones over benevolence, superiority over self-respect, and recognition over relationships.

Mary's confident words show not only that God has done these things in her life, but that she can also imagine this reality, God's reality, for others. To be sure, these words are for people who, in the world's eyes, are weak, powerless, and lowly. They also speak to people who have been shut down by others telling them what to think or how to feel, to times when truth has been determined by a so-called truth from the outside, and to moments when emptiness is the only thing you feel and you are really, truly convinced that you are inadequate. God is about transformation. God will lift us up, not into positions of power, but into living out who we are called to be.

Questions to Ponder

- Think of a time when God has lifted you up from a lowly place in your life. How was this a transformation for you?
- This Advent season, what is God calling you to do or to be?

Prayer

God of truth, you lift us up from those places where we feel like we are nothing. Help us remember that in our being raised up, you have given us a new chance to share ourselves, who we truly are, with the world. Amen.

Day 20: Friday

Food for the Hungry
Luke 1:46-55

 Key Verse: "He has filled the hungry with good things, and sent the rich away empty." Luke 1:53

Mary's song connects the dots between the God she knows and has always known, and the God who is orienting her future through her son. Her song foreshadows the life-changing experiences of characters who will encounter Jesus as the story unfolds. In a profound way, Mary realizes that God's favor of her will be experienced by others because of Jesus. Reading from the prophet Isaiah, Jesus in his first sermon establishes the connection between what God has done in the past and what God is now doing: "The Spirit of the Lord is upon me, because he has anointed me to bring good news to the poor. He has sent me to proclaim release to the captives and recovery of sight to the blind, to let the oppressed go free, to proclaim the year of the Lord's favor" (4:18-19). Further along in Luke's Gospel, Jesus says, "Blessed are you who are poor, for yours is the kingdom of God. Blessed are you who are hungry now, for you will be filled. Blessed are you who weep now, for you will laugh" (6:20-21). What God has done, Jesus will do as well.

We hear in Mary's song that God's mercy and favor satisfy her every hunger and need. God reaches out to fill those who hunger due to lack of food. How might we bring God's mercy and favor to people facing hunger, poverty, oppression, or grief? Mary points also to the hungers or needs we have because we are human. We hunger for sustenance, for belonging, for worthiness, for acknowledgment, for regard. We hunger too for companionship, for intimacy, for love. What might it mean to be filled with "good things" in these cases? How might we bring God's mercy and favor to people suffering from these types of hunger?

Questions to Ponder

- For what do you hunger? Where and how and through whom is God responding to your needs?
- Who might need you to bring them some kind of hope, comfort, or good news? Think of people nearby and far away, those you know and those you may never meet. In the next two weeks, what is one thing you can do to alleviate someone's hunger?

Prayer

God of fulfillment, in this season of Advent, send your Spirit upon us, that we might bring good news to the poor, proclaim release to the captives and recovery of sight to the blind, let the oppressed go free, and proclaim the year of the Lord's favor, all for the sake of ourselves and for the world. Amen.

Day 21: Saturday

Memory and Future

Luke 1:46-55

> 🔖 *Key Verse:* "He has helped his servant Israel, in remembrance of his mercy, according to the promise he made to our ancestors, to Abraham and to his descendants forever." Luke 1:54-55

Mary concludes her song with a confession or declaration of faith. Restating an opening theme to her song, that God is a saving God, she points to God's relationship with and mercy for Israel. To claim God as Savior is to know and believe in God's saving activity throughout the generations. Mary claims her own place in this history. She has received God's mercy, God's promises, and God's love, just like Abraham and Sarah. She is one of their descendants, and through her, their descendants will go on forever. God's mercy will go on forever too, as shown in the book of Acts, extending beyond the bounds of Israel to include all people, even those we deem as unworthy or outsiders. Mary can picture herself in this great cloud of witnesses. All of this is based on God's promise, which Mary knows to be absolutely true and certain.

Remembering is another theme in the song's conclusion. Remembrance calls upon events in time and rehearses how and why things happened the way they did. At the same time, the power of memory is capable of calling to mind a specific moment and the feelings that it created. Mary remembers what it was like to experience God's mercy and favor and to be on the receiving end of God's promises. What Mary has always known about God and God's mercy, help, presence, and steadfast love has become her actual experience. And now when we remember Mary, we remember God's mercy, favor, and promises. What God has done for her will never be forgotten.

Mary's song catapults us into the future. God's activity cannot and does not end with God's intervention in her life. Rather, she is a part of God's vision that extends beyond her, the people in her story, even beyond the ministry of Jesus himself. God's mercy cannot be stopped. It does not end when Luke ends. It does not end when Acts ends. Advent reminds us that this is just the beginning, the beginning of a new church year, the beginning of a new year in our relationship with God, another year of rejoicing in God our Savior.

Questions to Ponder

- How will you look for God's favor and blessing in your life in the new year?
- How might you witness to God's ongoing mercy in and for the world?

Prayer

God of hope, be present among us, not how we expect you to be but how you need to be and we need you to be. Help us to see your presence in our lives and in the world, that others might see in us your love and grace. Amen.

Week 4: Servant Song

Day 22: Sunday

Divine Descent

Philippians 2:5-8

> 🔲 *Key Verse:* Let the same mind be in you that was in Christ Jesus,
> who, though he was in the form of God, did not regard equality
> with God as something to be exploited, but emptied himself.
> Philippians 2:5-7a

How rare it is when someone in a position of privilege chooses to leave that place
for the sake of another! When politicians are running for office, they visit towns
and cities, eating the local fare. Though they meet the people, they are just pass-
ing through. Their purpose is to be elected. We watch to see if promises made in
our neighborhoods will be forgotten once we are out of sight. Striving for more
votes, more power, and more status is something we see regularly, even within
ourselves. So when a rare exception appears on the scene, it is worth noticing.

Paul, the writer of the letter to the Philippians, was a missionary who
preached and taught the good news of Jesus in many parts of the ancient Medi-
terranean world. While we elect our leaders and they must maintain at least a
pretense of interest in us, in Paul's time those born into lordship over a realm
needed only to attend to those above them and bow to their wishes. Looking
downward was rare; moving to be with those at the bottom was even rarer. So
when an alternative appeared, it was worth noting.

In Philippians Paul sings the praises of Christ Jesus, whose journey moves in
a different direction. Paul did not compose this hymn on his own. Rather, he bor-
rowed from a song loved by the faithful. Paul sings it into his letter in the same
way pastors sometimes find themselves quoting "O come, O come, Emmanuel"

during Advent sermons. Yet the rhythms of this servant song get stuck in Paul's head. As he muses on other subjects throughout this letter—imprisonment, the righteousness of faith, the joy that is ours, the mind-set that Christ creates in us—the themes of this song return.

While in popular imagination God is often seen as distant, shrouded with mystery, and endowed with unlimited power, Jesus acts in a way that challenges that mind-set. He redefines God by choosing the way of divine descent. He could have dwelt with God forever, staying in that place where he shared divine status. But he did not. Christ Jesus refused to make privilege into an eternal dwelling. He did not cling to, clutch, or exploit the place of glory, but rather chose to come down to us and share our lot. The one who was with God at the beginning of all creation took on the life of God's creatures. His infinity enclosed itself in our finite flesh. Not content with this, he descended to the bottom, to the place left for slaves. And he willingly died in the same horrible manner that escaped slaves suffered. His faithfulness defines God. God has come near; divine mystery is revealed as the mystery of love; all power is set aside to be vulnerably with us. This is worth noticing!

Questions to Ponder

- Think about someone who voluntarily left behind privilege or status. How rare is this in our world?
- How does this divine descent redefine God for you?

Prayer

Holy God, you have come down to be with us, to share our lot. Help us treasure the rare gift you offer us, in Christ Jesus. Amen.

Day 23: Monday

Divine Assent

Philippians 2:9-11

> 💬 *Key Verse:* Therefore God also highly exalted him and gave him the name that is above every name. Philippians 2:9

The second stanza of the hymn in Philippians 2 responds to the events already described in the first stanza (2:5-8). First Christ Jesus emptied himself of divine privilege; then God exalted him for that obedience. Christians may connect this pattern with the death and resurrection of Jesus. In fact, among the many ways the resurrection has been understood, one is that it is God's vindication of Jesus and all he proclaimed. The world's verdict on Jesus decreed that he was wrong and deserved to lose his life; God's verdict, put on display through the resurrection, is that Jesus got it all right and that he *is* life.

But notice the way the two stanzas of this hymn go together. What puts the name of Jesus on everyone's lips is the inspiring, self-sacrificing way he engaged the world. Jesus lived out the heart of divine desire by offering himself fully for all who had need. This self-giving, even all the way to death on the cross, is what causes others to praise him. Jesus is not worshiped because God bullies everyone into bowing down before him or suffering the consequences. Rather, Jesus lives out the divine vision of love in such a way that we find ourselves wanting to confess his name. In fact, our enthusiasm is so great it is celebrated above, upon, and even under the earth! God does not demand our respect of Jesus; Jesus' godly giving inspires our respect.

Jesus shows us what God cares about above all else. Even more, Jesus is divine care in action. Ancient Israel knew that the central event of the community's life was the exodus, when God led the people out of slavery. They remembered the Lord saying to Moses, "I have observed the misery of my people who are in Egypt; I have heard their cry on account of their taskmasters. Indeed, I know their sufferings, and I have come down to deliver them . . ." (Exodus 3:7-8a). Divine descent to be with a people in need has always been God's way, long before Jesus emptied himself into human flesh and was executed on a cross. The name of the God of the exodus was exalted because of this mercy and compassion. Jesus steps down into this godly pattern. Therefore his name too ascends with the name of the LORD. His ascent receives divine assent.

This is important because it shows that the descent of Jesus is not a blip on the screen charting God's relationship with the world and humankind. Jesus didn't grit his teeth to endure three decades of suffering to move on to eternal glory. Rather, Jesus shares in God's glory by constantly being vulnerable among us. He too is aware of our cries, sees our afflictions, knows our pain, and therefore comes down to deliver us. The exaltation of God happens because God comes to save us, and this fills us with such joy that our lips sing divine praises. Although Philippians 2:5-11 is sometimes called a "Christ hymn," it is more than that. In these words we praise the eternal pattern of one who always comes down to meet us.

Questions to Ponder

- What suffering do you trust that God sees and knows in the world today?
- What is the difference between demanding respect and inspiring it?

Prayer

Descending God, thank you for hearing, seeing, and knowing our plight. May your mercy be celebrated throughout all creation. Amen.

Day 24: Tuesday

Free in Christ

Philippians 1:12-18

Key Verse: It has become known throughout the whole imperial guard and to everyone else that my imprisonment is for Christ. Philippians 1:13

When bad things happen to me, I tend to take them personally. I fret and fume, getting all caught up in my own misery. How different is the take Paul has on his current suffering as he writes to believers in Philippi. He finds himself in prison—again. Though he was imprisoned unjustly each time, Colossians, Philemon, Ephesians, and Philippians all state that Paul is in jail. As he travels and proclaims the good news, bringing gospel freedom to people, others resent Paul and throw him in prison. But his letter to the Philippians shows no resentment about this. He rejoices throughout and invites his hearers to do the same. Why?

It all goes back to the hymn in Philippians 2. Paul is absolutely captivated by the one who was in the form of God, but came down to be among us and die with us. Paul sings this song with such fervor that it has taken over his life. His life is shaped like that of Christ Jesus. Paul sees his place in prison as a way to be conformed to God, who always and everywhere comes down in lowliness. Paul sees that his imprisonment allows him to make known the name of Jesus. Though he is in chains, the gospel has free course. Paul is so confident of this that the imperial guards take notice! Through Paul's imprisonment, Christ and his freedom are made known. Paul, like Jesus, lets go of a place of comfort and security that was his by right. He empties himself to the point that he is in chains awaiting his fate. Like Jesus, he has been judged wrong by the standards of the world in which he lived, but he awaits God's vindication and trusts that his emptying of himself is the way of exaltation.

Perhaps Paul had expected the worst from the Roman powers, and so he was ready for this huge infringement on his freedom. But he goes on to note that some people are preaching Christ out of rivalry, hoping to make Paul's situation worse. Yet even here Paul is joyful: Who cares why they preach, as long as Christ is made known?

Like Paul, we might have good cause to hold on to resentment. In relationships with family members and friends over the years, we are bound to have been hurt and to have hurt someone, making it difficult to gather together for Christmas or even contact each other by phone, text, or e-mail. What if this year we asked God to empty our hearts of resentment and help us find ways to share good news with others? We could let go of the old patterns that gnaw away at us and take on the pattern of Jesus in his self-emptying. We could join with Paul in singing with joyful hearts.

Questions to Ponder

· What do you make of Paul's rejoicing while in chains?
· What do you need to let go of so that others might have life?

Prayer

God with us, we let ourselves go down into your supporting arms that you might lift us up and show us the high road to take. In Jesus' name. Amen.

Day 25: Wednesday

Surpassing Gift

Philippians 3:3-11

Key Verse: More than that, I regard everything as loss because of the surpassing value of knowing Christ Jesus my Lord. Philippians 3:8a

Some gifts are easy to set aside. We open a gift, stare in confusion, and wonder if the giver knows us at all. We put it in the "re-gift" pile in a closet and forget about it. After some time has passed, we give the gift to someone else (who may not want it either).

When Paul speaks about the many talents, gifts, and claims that have mattered to him in the past, he is not talking about things he can easily set aside. They are not ill-chosen or unsuitable, but things he has carried with him in his travels. They provide him with status and esteem within his community. His body was marked with the sign of God's covenant; he is part of God's chosen people; even within this group he is a member of the Pharisees, known for their dedication to God's way. He has followed the ways of the law. All these claims matter to Paul. At least they did until something happened to eclipse even the greatest of these gifts in Paul's heart.

Jesus showed up, having emptied himself, and he embraced Paul not because Paul was so faithful, but because Jesus is. And having seen Jesus, who emptied himself of all the rights that come with divinity, Paul emptied himself of all the rights that come with living righteously, in order to be right by Christ's side. Three times in Philippians 3:7-11 Paul speaks of letting go of the things that were most precious in his sight, so that his hands will be free and ready to cling completely to Jesus: "Whatever gains I had, these I have come to regard as loss because of Christ. . . . I regard everything as loss because of the surpassing value of knowing Christ Jesus my Lord. For his sake I have suffered the loss of all things, and I regard them as rubbish." What makes Paul do this?

A child has opened gift after gift, thrilled that her requests have been heard. Each gift a desire fulfilled. Sitting among her toys, she looks up and out the window to see her daddy and mommy walking up the driveway leading a pony. She had wanted a pony, but never even dared to ask or to hope for a gift that tremendous. She leaps over the building blocks and doll and guitar she requested, forgetting them in the excitement of seeing a gift she never could have anticipated. This is beyond wonderful. Trusting that this gift is for her, she leaves behind all that had been precious to her in order to tell about and share this surprising gift with everyone within range!

Paul was surrounded with the cherished blessings his people had received. But when Jesus showed up, God surprised him. His heart was captured, and nothing else mattered as in faith he took hold of the new gift God brought him. He emptied himself of all else to share with the world the new surprise offered in Jesus.

Questions to Ponder

·   What are the precious gifts we let go of because of the surpassing greatness made present in Jesus?
·   What does trust or faith in Jesus mean to you?

Prayer

Surprising God, wow! Thank you. Amen.

Day 26: Thursday

Another Citizenship

Philippians 3:20—4:1

Key Verse: But our citizenship is in heaven, and it is from there that we are expecting a Savior, the Lord Jesus Christ. Philippians 3:20

Citizenship is a serious issue in any time and place. It comes with rights and privileges; it binds you to a whole group of people who share those rights and privileges. If someone comes from another land and makes our nation her own, we insist that she swear her loyalty to her new nation with a pledge of allegiance. We want to know that should a crisis arise, she will be on our side and we can count on her to stand for the things we care about most deeply.

Paul does not take citizenship lightly when he says our citizenship is not in this world, but in heaven. He shows where our ultimate allegiance must lie. If times of crisis arise, and he knows they will on a daily basis, we must be clear about whose side we are on and what stand we will take. Our heavenly citizenship is formally like that of national citizenship, but that is where the similarity ends. We understand our rights and responsibilities as citizens by looking to the one whose own heavenly citizenship is beyond question, Jesus Christ. He is the Savior who comes from heaven so that where he is there we shall be also. Like the first family member who goes ahead of the others to a new country, he has gone ahead of us and is preparing a place for us. As members of his family, we will share in his status. In heaven we too shall belong.

Until that day when we go to be where he is, we are practicing the customs and values of that place so that we arrive at life eternal, ready to give all that we are. So now we listen carefully to the Word he sends us, to learn to speak in its cadences. We anticipate the feast of great belonging by eating together at a table that knows no boundaries. Christ joins us in our present humiliation so that we also will join him in his glory. Yet because true citizenship with Jesus is modeled after his example, we know that in radical ways it will be unlike citizenship in any earthly nation. He does not demand strong borders to keep out the riffraff, but tells us to bring along all who would join us. He tells us not to fear that the resources will be scarce where he is, but to practice generosity to any who might have a need. And when a crisis arises, he does not call us to arms to do violence to our enemies; rather he stretches out his arms to remind us of the response he gave to his enemies from the cross.

Throughout the ages, God has raised up those who lived in this world as if they were already in the next. Paul broke down some of the fundamental barriers that had divided one people from another. Francis embraced poverty and the poor, letting go of his family's great wealth. Katie left the surety of the convent to embrace God's calling to serve the world. What heavenly citizens have you noticed?

Questions to Ponder

- What role does your citizenship play in shaping your values?
- Where does your national citizenship clash with the heavenly one that Paul calls us to embrace?

Prayer

Holy God, you welcome us into a far-off country where we shall dwell for eternity. You welcome us now to prepare our hearts and values for the newness that awaits us. Amen.

Day 27: Friday

The God of Peace

Philippians 4:8-9

> *Key Verse:* Keep on doing the things that you have learned and received and heard and seen in me, and the God of peace will be with you. Philippians 4:9

As the movie *Elf* (New Line Cinema, 2003) returns to the holiday film queues, many will smile as Buddy comes spinning into his biological father's office, saying, "I'm in love, I'm in love, and I don't care who knows it!" He interrupts business as usual to celebrate the new relationship that is suddenly blooming. Gone are his confusion at being in a strange place, his pain at being rebuffed by the father he had thought would welcome him, and his struggles with his identity, given what life has dealt him. The new love dawning on the horizon reframes all of the many challenges that threaten him. Being loved and loving another transforms everything.

In this week's reflections, we see Paul spinning into the Philippian community and declaring the love he has found in Christ Jesus. The apostle has known his own forms of confusion, pain, and identity struggles, but in Christ he is given enough security to not be overwhelmed by everything else that screams out for his attention. He tells believers in Philippi that even as they face multiple issues demanding resolution, the essential, first thing to do is to rejoice in the Lord who has come down to embrace them. Secure in this knowledge they can turn to those around them (is he perhaps thinking of the more difficult members of the community?) with gentleness and patience. So many fruits are already growing on the tree of life that Jesus has planted with them. They are joyful; they live with gentleness toward those around them; they will be thankful toward God for what they have received. Then, having discovered how trustworthy God is, so they know they are free to share all their concerns and sorrows, they can place the many issues of their lives in God's capable hands. Finally, the peace of God that goes far beyond any means we have to explain it will hover over their hearts and their minds, offering security and protection in Christ Jesus.

Paul continues explaining to the Philippian Christians the best way to tend these precious fruits that God is causing to grow among them. They are to set their attention upon all that is good and life-giving in their midst. Paul lays out a thorough description of the things that are worthy of their attention and ours. Think on those things, he says, that are true, honorable, just, pure, pleasing, commendable, excellent, and worthy of praise. This naturally will pull them away from what is false, dishonorable, unjust, impure, disgusting, lamentable, mediocre, and unworthy. When Paul calls for this change of focus for the mind and heart, he trusts it will lead to a new direction in the way they live their lives as well. These virtues are not only ideas; they are things Christians are called to enact. We are to live authentically, not dishonoring others but seeking justice for them. We are to turn from all that is shabby and therefore cheapens life. The peace God offers us as a gift, with generous hands extended, becomes something even greater. For we find we have more than the peace of God. The gift is quickly surpassed by the self-offering of the Giver! The peace of God becomes the direct embrace of the God of peace. Life cannot be business as usual any longer. We spin in the joyful knowledge, saying, "We are in love and want everyone to know!"

Questions to Ponder

- Have you ever seen someone transformed by being in love?
- What are the things on which you will set your heart and mind this day?

Prayer

Holy God, it would have been enough for you to offer us your peace, but you surpassed all that we could ever hope for by giving us yourself as well. Move us to rejoice in your embrace. Amen.

Day 28: Saturday

Humming Along

Philippians 2:1-5

🔳 *Key Verse:* Let the same mind be in you that was in Christ Jesus.
Philippians 2:5

"If" was a word I dreaded as a child. Before I had taken a single class in grammar, I understood what "if" meant. I understood its conditional nature. I could go to my friend's house *if* I cleaned my room. I would get a ride to the event *if* someone was available to take me. We would go to the movie *if* we could demonstrate that we could get along. I knew that *if* signaled a big maybe, and when the conditions looked all but unlikely, it could be taken as a "No!" The sense of give-and-take implied in that tiny word is important. I have passed it on to my own children, even though I know that *if* is shaky ground upon which to build a foundation.

Paul begins Philippians 2:1-5 with a series chock full of that little word. The NRSV is gentle with us; perhaps the translators had heard Paul's call to gentleness in Philippians 4:5. They reduce Paul's repetition of "if" from four times to only one. But the Greek text forces readers to wonder if they should hope against hope: If there is encouragement, if there is consolation, if there is sharing, if there is compassion and sympathy . . . Sometimes I look around at faith communities in all our imperfection, and the absence of encouragement, sharing, and sympathy drives me to despair. In these real-world situations, Paul's conditionals seem less like maybe and more like an outright no. Yet Paul believes his joy will be made complete by the Philippians. What is the source of this untamed hope?

While we cannot by our own reason or effort come up with encouragement, consolation, sharing, and compassion, Paul declares that we have already been shown and given these gifts in Christ. In fact, he reminds us to remake our minds. When we remember that Christ came to us while we were deep in despair, we find ourselves equipped to encourage others. When we remember the consolation poured out upon us in Christ's descent, we find consolation flowing through us toward those who grieve. When we remember that Christ came down to share our lot in life and even in death, we know the freedom that breaks down barriers and allows us to share with other members of our community. When we recall that Christ has shown us compassion, we find ourselves humming along with his song sympathetically. When we have Christ making our minds new, we find our minds shaped by his cross after his pattern. Nothing is more important than the one who went down lower than all else so that we might have peace, salvation, and life.

We are on the brink of celebrating Christ's descent to be with us. Let us set our hearts on his gift of himself, that we may find ourselves members of a community that conforms to his pattern. We will not agree upon every point; in fact, we will disagree about things each of us believes matter a great deal. But if we set our minds and hearts on what is true, excellent, and worthy of praise, that is, if we stake our lives on Christ Jesus, we will share encouragement, compassion, and love—no ifs, maybes, or buts about it.

Questions to Ponder

- What are the conditions that seem to block your community from fully realizing the future God has prepared for you?
- How will you bring forward Christ's encouragement, consolation, and compassion in the week ahead?

Prayer

Your glory, O Christ, is shown in your willingness to go all the way down even to death itself. Help us die with you to all that blocks your compassion, that we may rise with you to serve our neighbor in need. Amen.

Bible Studies

Bible Study: Week 1

God's New Song

Job 38:4-7	Luke 2:13-14
John 1:1-14	Luke 10:38-42
Revelation 5:8-14	

"Sing to the LORD, bless his name; tell of his salvation from day to day," says Psalm 96. This song of faith is our response to the Lord's song of creation and salvation, the song of grace that begins everything. It is the LORD who holds our world together and who will make all things new. Listen and let these lyrics of good news sink deep into you; then sing and share the song with others so the chorus of faith and witness may grow.

1. The book of Job tells about one man's adversities and the questions raised during his suffering. Read part of God's response to these questions in Job 38:4-7. How are Job's questions answered? Take a moment to contemplate the greatness of the Lord and creation, when even "the morning stars sang together." What words would you use to describe the power and beauty of God?

2. The angels sing God's song in the dark of night for a group of lowly shepherds. Imagine that you are one of those shepherds as you read Luke 2:13-14 aloud. How would you react to this heavenly chorus? Would you tell others what you've heard this night? How would you do this?

_____

_____

3. God's song comes to us in Jesus. Read John 1:1-14 and write down any words or phrases that grab your attention. Where or how is Jesus coming to you this Advent?

_____

_____

_____

4. Everyday tasks and worries can keep us from focusing on God's song. Read Luke 10:38-42. What tasks and worries distract you from Jesus? When do you sit at his feet? This Advent, how will you focus on what God has done, is doing, and will do?

_____

_____

_____

5. God's song is eternal. Read Revelation 5:8-14. How does this vision give you hope? How will you sing or share God's song in your life?

_____

_____

_____

Bible Study: Week 2

Song of Light

Isaiah 42:1-9

By now Christmas lights brighten the darkness. Children are getting excited about gifts under the tree. Christmas parties are being held. We can feel the anticipation in the air. Yet even in the midst of this excitement, the powerful words from Isaiah 42 draw us back to the cross, back to Jesus' suffering, dying, and rising. All of life is lived in the shadow of the cross. So we sing songs of light in the darkness of December. We sing with hope grounded in the promise of grace coming to us through Jesus. We sing with joy, for his coming is certain.

1. The words of Isaiah 42 promise the servant will bring justice. Where do you long to see justice in your life? What would justice look like? Where do we need to see justice in the world? How would a just world be different from the world as it is today?

2. Songs help both children and adults learn the faith. Review Isaiah 42:1-9. What songs come to mind? What do those songs teach about faith? (You might start with "Amazing Grace, How Sweet the Sound" [ELW 779], which includes the words "[I] was blind but now I see"). What songs and hymns give you hope and strengthen your faith?

3. Isaiah 42:5 reminds us that creation comes as a gift from God. What is your favorite place in creation? Do you have a special vacation spot? Where do you find peace?

_____

_____

_____

4. In Isaiah 42:7 God promises "to bring out . . . from the prison those who sit in darkness." Think of those who are alone or lonely: people homebound, hospitalized, or grieving the loss of a loved one. How are you called to sing the light of Christ into their lives?

_____

_____

_____

5. The words from Isaiah bring to mind Jesus and his suffering on the cross. Consider crosses you have seen. Some crosses are ornate, others are simple. Which crosses speak most meaningfully to you?

_____

_____

_____

Bible Study: Week 3

Mary's Song

Luke 1

Advent, as the beginning of a new church year, provides us an opportunity to think about what is most important to us when it comes to our relationship with God, with one another, and even with ourselves. Mary's song gives voice to these important matters. As this new church year begins, rather than focusing on all of the things you want to change about yourself or all of the Christmas preparations you do not seem to be getting done, consider thinking about the good things God has given you and how you will carry Mary's song into your life and into the world.

1. Scan all of Luke 1 and identify some of the themes in this chapter. How has God shown mercy and faithfulness? How would you describe God's faithfulness in your life?

2. Read Luke 1:46-55. What in Mary's song affects you most deeply, and why?

3. Reflect on this translation of Luke 1:46-48: "I'm bursting with God-news; I'm dancing the song of my Savior God. God took one good look at me, and look what happened—I'm the most fortunate woman on earth. What God has done for me will never be forgotten" (Eugene H. Peterson, *The Message: The Bible in Contemporary Language*). How do you experience Mary's words differently in this translation?

_____

_____

_____

4. Rewrite Mary's song in your own words. Draw on your experiences and use your own language to personalize this passage for you. Save what you write so that you can return to it when you need to be lifted up.

_____

_____

_____

_____

Bible Study: Week 4

Servant Song

Philippians 2:5-11

In Philippians 2, the apostle Paul sings a song about the mystery of a love that sets power aside to be with us. Christ Jesus did not cling to, clutch, or exploit the place of glory, but chose to come down to us and share our lot as human beings. More than that, he descended even further and willingly died in the horrible manner often suffered by escaped slaves in the Roman Empire. Nothing is more important than this Jesus, who went down lower than all else so that *we* might have peace, salvation, and life.

1. Read Philippians 2:5-11. What key dynamics do you see in the faithful pattern that Jesus reveals in this hymn?

2. What words stand out to you in the lyrics of this song? What about Jesus surprises or amazes you here?

3. In what ways could this hymn help us reimagine the way we celebrate Christ's descent to be with us? Look through the Christmas songs section of ELW for hymns that reflect the song in Philippians 2. What do they claim happens at

Jesus' birth? What other themes arise in these hymns that complement Paul's theme of divine descent?

_____

_____

_____

4. Think about a community of faith that has meaningfully witnessed to God's compassion. Describe a particular moment when you saw members of that community living in conformity to the pattern of life Jesus exhibits in this hymn. What were the circumstances that required consolation and sympathy? What specific things did people do that made them of one mind?

_____

_____

_____

5. Name elements of your congregation's life together that are cause for rejoicing and hope. Identify one way to share your observations with those who have exercised their gifts to build up the church.

_____

_____

_____

6. Pray for those who have studied with you during this Advent season. Have half the group close their eyes while the other group moves from person to person laying on hands and silently praying for the God of peace in their lives, then switch roles.

Activities

Week 1: God's New Song

Advent Blessings Wreath (week 1 of 4)

At the start of this Advent season, plan to spend a few moments as a family each week (more often, if you can) focusing on the many blessings you receive from God and the things you do to share God's blessings with family members, friends, coworkers, and people you meet. Assemble your Advent Blessings Wreath in the first week and add to it throughout the season.

Materials needed: A wire wreath form, wooden clothespins, green and red acrylic paint and brushes or green and red paint pens, newspaper, black fine-tip markers, a basket or box, a media player and favorite seasonal music, a bow for the wreath (optional)

Time required: 15–20 minutes (initial preparation time includes painting the clothespins)

1. Play your favorite seasonal music softly in the background. Talk together about the season of Advent and what it means to your family. How does your family have fun spending time together during the days and weeks leading up to Christmas?

2. Spread the newspaper out on a table and lay the clothespins on it. Have fun together painting the majority or two-thirds of the clothespins green, and the rest of the clothespins red.

3. As you are working, talk about the ways God blesses each of you and your family.

4. Add a bow to the wire wreath form at this time or wait until Christmas Eve or Christmas Day.

5. Hang the wreath, at a height everyone can reach, in a central place in your home. Store the dry, painted clothespins nearby in the basket or box. Encourage everyone to clip a clothespin onto the wreath during the week whenever they notice a blessing from God. If they like, they can write these blessings on the clothespins with a marker.

6. Whenever you gather together near the wreath for a time of Advent family devotions, recognize the growing number of clothespins filling out the wreath.

All the Earth Desktop Terrarium

O sing to the LORD a new song; sing to the LORD, all the earth. Psalm 96:1

Materials needed: Glass jar, bowl, or container; horticultural charcoal (available at most garden or nursery centers); pebbles or small rocks; pieces of tree bark or other natural items; potting soil; one or more small plants; a long spoon or chopstick; water; newspaper; fine-tip marker; small dowel or stick; cardstock or heavy paper; tape or glue

Time required: 15–20 minutes

1. Cover a desk or table with newspaper. Clean and dry your glass container.

2. Layer these items in the container in this order: charcoal to cover the bottom of the container, small pebbles or rocks, and potting soil.

3. Carefully remove the small plants from their pots, leaving some soil on the roots. Press the plant roots into place in the container, adding more soil and tamping down to hold the plants upright and in place. A long spoon or chopstick can be helpful to move plants or to tamp down the soil.

4. Once you are happy with the plant placement, you may want to add small rocks, pieces of tree bark, or other natural items to the terrarium.

5. Print Psalm 96:1 in very small letters on a slip of cardstock or paper, and attach with tape or glue to the top of the small dowel or stick. Add this "signpost" to your terrarium.

6. Water lightly and set your terrarium on a desk or table that gets some natural light each day. Enjoy this little bit of nature even during the dark and cold days of winter.

Family Tree

Seasons change. People grow and change. Even trees grow and change! A photo op illustrating this growth can be a great reminder of the blessings you have living as a family together in God's unchanging love!

Materials needed: Digital camera, a four-part photo frame or four matching frames, a favorite tree

Time required: 10 minutes

1. Find a favorite tree that can serve as the centerpiece of a family photo. (Is there a special tree nearby, maybe one your family planted? Do you have a favorite tree someplace in your community where you like to go as a family?)

2. Gather everyone near this tree and take a family photo. To get everyone in the photo, use a timer or invite a friend to be your photographer.

3. Plan to go back and photograph your family with the same tree three more times in the next year—in the spring, summer, and fall. Mark the dates on your calendar.

4. As the tree grows and changes in your photos, consider the ways your family has grown and changed as well.

5. When you print and frame your photos, be sure to label them with the dates and names of family members.

Paint-Chip Mosaic

God's creation is a mosaic of so many different things! Make your own mosaics of your favorite people and places in God's world or of what you see every day!

Materials needed: Assorted colors of paint-chip samples or scrapbook, wallpaper, construction paper, or colorful magazine pages; scissors; pencil or pen; glue; markers; thin cardboard or poster board

Time required: 30–45 minutes

1. Think about what you want to create for your mosaic. Will your family work together on a design, or will each person create their own?

2. Draw a simple outline of your design on the thin cardboard or poster board. Don't add too much detail, as it could be difficult to duplicate in a mosaic.

3. Cut the paint chips or sheets of paper into pieces at least 1" square (prepare these squares ahead of time for small children). You might want to sort pieces by color to make it easier to work with them.

4. Lay mosaic pieces on your design. Some mosaics have a border around each piece, while others are glued right next to one another. Your design will help you decide which method you will use.

5. When you are pleased with the way your mosaic looks, carefully glue the pieces in place.

6. Find a place of honor for displaying your mosaic in your home!

"I Spy" Bottle

How often do we stop and take the time to really examine the world around us and all that we see in it? Have a little fun making this "I Spy" bottle, then keep it on your kitchen counter, coffee table, or even in the car, as a reminder to stop and look every day!

Materials needed: One clean, unbreakable bottle, a funnel, birdseed, strapping tape, small items that will fit into the bottle (small plastic toys or game pieces, miniature nature items such as pebbles and pinecones, and so on)

Time required: 10 minutes

1. Wash and dry an unbreakable bottle that has a screw-type cap. Gather small items that will fit through the neck of the bottle and are reminders of creation and God's love, or mementos of vacations, trips, or time your family has spent together.

2. Use the funnel to fill the bottle half full with birdseed, then alternate slipping the small items you have collected into the bottle in between additional amounts of birdseed.

3. Twist, turn, and shake the bottle while adding items to make sure they are evenly distributed among the seed.

4. Continue this process until the bottle is full, then screw on the top securely.

5. Note: If you have small children who may be tempted to unscrew the bottle cap, reinforce the closure with strapping tape.

6. To use the "I Spy" bottle, everyone can take turns turning and twisting it to see how many items they discover inside.

Week 2: Song of Light

Advent Blessings Wreath (week 2 of 4)

Keep adding to your blessings wreath in this second week of Advent.

Materials needed: The wire wreath and clothespins prepared in Week 1; if you are preparing this project this week, you will need: a wire wreath form, wooden clothespins, green and red acrylic paint and brushes or green and red paint pens, newspaper, black fine-tip markers, a basket or box, a media player and favorite seasonal music, a bow for the wreath (optional)

Time required: 10–15 minutes

1. Set up your music and have it playing softly in the background as you gather with your family near your wreath. Begin with a simple prayer thanking God for your family and for this time when you can be together.

2. Talk about the many ways God has blessed you this week. Give everyone a few moments to tell about blessings they added to the wreath, or to add a blessing clothespin now.

3. One way we can share God's blessings is by praying for others. For the week ahead, think about individuals, families, and groups of people who might be in need of prayer at this time. These might be people nearby or far away, some you know very well and others you will never meet.

4. Write the names of people you will pray for on the clothespins, and pin them to the wreath. Invite everyone to add names throughout the week and to include these people in their daily prayers.

Jigsaw Star Ornaments

Sometimes it is easier to see the stars at night at this time of the year, when the sky tends to be darker. Let these star ornaments remind your family to take time to look at the stars during this Advent season and enjoy this wonderful part of God's creation.

Materials needed: Old jigsaw puzzle pieces, gold or silver acrylic paint, gold or silver glitter, wooden craft sticks, glue, paintbrush or cotton swabs, wax paper, jingle bells, ribbon, scissors

Time required: 30 minutes plus drying time

1. Collect old jigsaw puzzle pieces.

2. Lay wax paper on the table and paint the puzzle pieces with gold or silver paint.

3. Crisscross four wooden craft sticks together in the center, making a pointed star shape.

4. Start gluing puzzle pieces onto the craft sticks, first covering the base of the sticks, then overlapping the pieces on top of each other to build depth and dimension.

5. When you are happy with the puzzle-piece placement, make sure the pieces are glued firmly to the sticks. Then use the brush or cotton swab to spread a thin layer of glue over the pieces and sprinkle glitter on them.

6. Tie a piece of ribbon at the top of the star for hanging on your Christmas tree as an ornament or in your window.

Mission Map Prayers

God's people live all around the world, and every day there are people and places in the news that can use our prayers.

Materials needed: A large map of your city, state, country, or the world; a small notebook and pen; access to a daily newspaper (print or online)

Time required: 10 minutes

1. Find a central place in your home to post a map of your city, state, country, or even the world.

2. Designate a small notebook and pen as your Mission Map Prayer Notebook. Keep it near the map, along with the daily newspaper.

3. When you gather together for family time, or throughout the week whenever someone in the family has an opportunity, take a look at the current news of the world. What people or places could use your prayers? Jot down the names, places, events, or dates in the Mission Map Prayer Notebook.

4. Encourage everyone in the family to use this notebook listing as a springboard for prayer time, together or privately.

Canning Jar Luminaries

Your word is a lamp to my feet and a light to my path. Psalm 119:105

A luminary can be used inside or outside to light your way. In the midst of winter, it is good to have light! How is God like your light when the world is dark around you?

Materials needed: a canning jar, small clear glass votive candleholder, votive candle or tea light (battery-operated if you wish), short string of battery-operated lights, metallic tinsel or garland, fine-tip pen, assorted embellishments such as ribbon, raffia, keys, buttons, and manila tags

Time required: 10 minutes

1. Make sure your jar is clean and dry. The votive candleholder should nest in the open top of the jar. (These instructions are for one luminary; consider making several as gifts or to line a driveway or sidewalk.)

2. Fill the jar with the tinsel or garland. If you are using a string of lights, arrange it inside the jar among the garland.

3. Set the votive candleholder in the top of the jar and place a candle or tea light inside it.

4. Wrap and tie the ribbon, raffia, twine, or other stringy things around the neck of the jar and attach buttons, keys, or other embellishments.

5. Print Psalm 119:105 on a manila tag and tie it onto the luminary as a reminder that God is always our light!

Metal Embossed Star

God loves us and asks us to love one another and to share the light of God's love in the world we live in. Make this special star to hang on your family's Christmas tree or on a doorknob in your home as a reminder to shine God's light of love in the world.

Materials needed: Paper; pencils; aluminum foil or other metal paper; a star template or pattern; scissors; masking tape; embossing tool or pen; paper hole punch; tracing tool (such as a dressmaker's wheel); newspaper, gold; silver, or copper acrylic paint, wax, or rubbing paste; thin ribbon

Time required: 15 minutes

1. Cut a piece of paper into a square slightly larger than you want your star to be.

2. Draw a star pattern on your square of paper. You may want to make a design inside your star, such as radiating lines or hearts.

3. Tear off a piece of aluminum foil and fold it a few times to create a square the same size as your piece of paper (if you are using a heavier sheet of metal that can be embossed without tearing, simply cut the metal sheet to the size of your paper).

4. Tape the paper onto the foil and trace the star shape with the embossing tool or pen to make an embossed or indented star on the foil.

5. Carefully cut the star from the folded aluminum foil. Punch a hole at the top point of the star.

6. Place the star you have cut on the newspaper and use the tracing tool or dressmaker's wheel to carefully press all the way around the star edge to make a dotted or dashed design. Then use the tracing tool or dressmaker's wheel on any designs you drew inside the star.

7. Use your finger to rub a bit of metallic paint, wax, or rubbing paste over the embossed star design. Your goal is to have the raised design stand out from the rest of the star.

8. When the paint dries, tie a piece of ribbon through the star for hanging on your Christmas tree.

9. An alternative to using the embossed star as a Christmas tree ornament is to make many more stars to use as decorations on your Christmas cards, packages, or letters. You can reuse the design you drew or create new designs.

Week 3: Mary's Song

Advent Blessings Wreath (week 3 of 4)

Make sure you have clothespins ready to add to your blessings wreath this week.

Materials needed: The wire wreath and clothespins prepared in Week 1; if you are preparing this project this week, you will need: a wire wreath form, wooden clothespins, green and red acrylic paint and brushes or green and red paint pens, newspaper, black fine-tip markers, a basket or box, a media player and favorite seasonal music, a bow for the wreath (optional)

Time required: 10–15 minutes

1. As the seasonal music plays softly, gather everyone together near your clothespin wreath. If you have run out of available clothespins, be sure to paint more before you meet. Pray a simple prayer together, asking God to bless your time and your life together as a family and to help you share the joy and peace that come from belonging to the family of God.

2. Talk about the wreath and note how many clothespins have been added in the past week. Wow, is the wreath filling up with green? It is fun to add some red clothespins to the wreath too, to represent the "holly berries" we often see on an evergreen wreath.

3. Discuss what it was like to pray for others during the week. Take time for everyone to add clothespins to the wreath if they have not done so already.

4. For the week ahead, talk about other ways you could share God's blessings with others. Do you have a special family cookie recipe you could bake and share with others? Is there a family member who could use the surprise of a clean car in the morning? Do you know a family in need that could use your

help right now? Could you invite a neighbor or friend to come to a worship service with you?

5. Invite everyone to add clothespins to the wreath during the week when they do or say something to share God's blessings with others.

Letter Tile Family Name Magnets

An angel visited Mary and told her she would have a baby boy who should be named Jesus. The name *Jesus* means "the Lord saves" in Hebrew. Who named you? What does your name mean?

Materials needed: Letter tiles such as Scrabble® letters, wooden craft sticks, craft glue or a hot glue gun and glue sticks, magnets

Time required: 10 minutes plus drying time

1. Collect letter tiles to use, such as Scrabble® or other board game letters.

2. Use letter tiles to arrange your name on a wooden craft stick. When the tiles are arranged on the stick as you want, glue them down.

3. When the glue has dried, glue a magnet to the back of the craft stick.

4. Use your name magnets to post notices on your file cabinet or refrigerator.

Cheerio! Feed the Birds

Attract birds to your home and find out how many songs they sing.

Materials needed: Floral wire, wire clippers, circle-shaped dry cereal (such as Cheerios®), twine or string, heart- or star-shaped cookie cutters (optional)

Time required: 15 minutes

1. Cut a piece of floral wire approximately 12" long. Twist one end into a loop to keep the cereal from sliding off the end.

2. Gently guide the wire into the shape of a heart or a star, using a cookie cutter for a form if you like.

3. Thread the circle-shaped cereal onto the wire until it is almost full.

4. Cross one end of the wire over the other. Twist the ends together to keep the cereal in place, completing the heart or star shape.

5. Tie a length of twine or string at the top of the heart or star for hanging.

6. Hang your wired bird feeder. What kinds of birds do you see? What songs do they sing?

You Shall Have a Song

Create your own family music "mix" to share with one another.

Materials needed: Your family's favorite music source and equipment

Time required: 30–60 minutes

1. What kinds of music does your family like to listen to? Does everyone like the same music or are there varied tastes in the music everyone plays at your house?

2. Use your favorite music and sources to make your own family music "mix" to share. Include at least one of each person's favorite songs.

3. Listen to this playlist as you enjoy some time together as a family. You might want to dance or sing along to the songs.

Hot Cocoa Marshmallow Dippers

Mmmm . . . is there anything better on a cold and blustery winter day than a nice cuppa hot cocoa? With whipped cream and sprinkles? Well, yes, maybe there is—if you have a marshmallow dipper to stir with! Be sure to make enough of these to share or to give as gifts.

Materials needed: Large marshmallows, peppermint sticks, melting chocolate (white or brown almond bark), sprinkles, chopped nuts, small bowls, microwave, glass bowl, wooden spoon, spatula, wax paper, paper cups, cups of hot cocoa

Time required: 15 minutes

1. Melt the chocolate in the glass bowl in the microwave according to the package directions. Stir often to make sure it melts evenly.

2. While the chocolate is melting, push one peppermint stick into each large marshmallow.

3. Lay a sheet of wax paper on the kitchen counter. Put sprinkles and chopped nuts into the small bowls.

4. When the chocolate is melted, dip each marshmallow into it, turning the peppermint stick to make sure that at least half of the marshmallow is covered in chocolate. Then dip the marshmallows into the bowls of sprinkles and chopped nuts to add a little extra sweetness to this hot cocoa treat!

5. Balance the marshmallow dippers on top of the paper cups to cool and harden.

6. Stir your hot cocoa with a dipper and enjoy!

Week 4: Servant Song

Advent Blessings Wreath (week 4 of 4)

As you fill out your wreath this week, think about all the blessings God has shared with you and you have shared with others.

Materials needed: The wire wreath and clothespins prepared in Week 1; if you are preparing this project this week, you will need: a wire wreath form, wooden clothespins, green and red acrylic paint and brushes or green and red paint pens, newspaper, black fine-tip markers, a basket or box, a media player and favorite seasonal music, a bow for the wreath (optional)

Time required: 10–15 minutes

1. If you have run out of available clothespins, be sure to paint more before you meet.

2. Gather everyone together and play some favorite seasonal music. Pray together, thanking and praising God for your family, for this special season of focusing on God's blessings and gifts to us, and for the most important gift of all—Jesus, God's own Son.

3. Talk about the many ways you have shared God's blessings and love with others in the past week. What was this like? Take time for everyone to add clothespins to the wreath if they have not done so already.

4. Invite everyone to continue adding clothespins to the wreath during the week when they do or say something to share God's blessings with others.

5. Close by singing a favorite Christmas song together.

Family Photo Cross

The baby Jesus was placed in a feed box, and a bunch of lowly shepherds were his first visitors. Use this family photo cross as a reminder that Jesus came to be one of us and went all the way to the cross to show how much God loves us.

Materials needed: Two thin pieces of wood, such as two paint-stir sticks or two wooden rulers, saw, family photos, paper, pencil, scissors, glue

Time required: 20 minutes

1. Lay the wood pieces in a cross shape to determine how much you will need to cut off of one of them for the horizontal crosspiece. If you are using paint sticks or rulers that have a hole on one end, lay out your pieces so that a hole is at the top of the cross for hanging.

2. Measure the wooden pieces to determine how big you will want to cut your photo pieces. Make a paper template approximately this size, then trace the portions of the photos you want to use. Leave a slight overlap between each photo to make the final cross smooth.

3. Cut the photos and glue them to the vertical and horizontal cross pieces. Be sure to check the placement so you don't cover up one of your photos when you assemble the two pieces together. Let the glue dry.

4. Glue the two cross pieces together and let dry.

5. Hang your family photo cross in a central gathering place or near your entry door.

Soup Mix Magic

There are many sources for soup mixes in a jar, and you may already have a favorite. Mix up some soup mix for your family, good friends, or neighbors and share the jar during this busy time of the year.

Materials needed: canning jars and lids, soup mix ingredients of your choice, raffia or ribbon, gift tags, measuring cups and spoons, a large bowl and mixing spoon

Time required: 30 minutes

1. Search for soup-in-a-jar recipes online. Choose a recipe and purchase the ingredients.

2. Make sure your jars and lids are clean and dry, then follow soup-mix directions and mix or layer in the jar as suggested.

3. When the jar is full, put on the lid and add a tag that includes the name of the soup as well as the entire recipe for completing the soup. Decorate the jar by adding raffia, twine, ribbon, or other embellishments.

4. Share with someone who could use a good bowl of soup!

Button Ornaments

Button, button . . . who's got a button? Most of us have a few unused buttons lying around, so use them to make ornaments for the Christmas tree!

Materials needed: Assorted buttons, depending on which type of ornament you will make; floral wire or long twist ties; ribbon; scissors

Time required: 10–15 minutes

1. Decide what type of ornament you would like to make with your buttons. The general directions here are for a tree or a wreath, but you can also just string buttons to make a garland or other objects of your choosing.

2. **Wreath:** Cut a length of wire that will make a wreath in the size you would like. A 3" diameter wreath is a good size to begin with. String the buttons onto the wire in a pattern or by color from dark to light—whatever you choose. If you want to have an accent piece in the center of your wreath (for example, if you are using green buttons and want to have one red button mark the center) be sure to slide that button on at the halfway point of your wire. Twist the wire ends together when you are done, then tie a piece of ribbon where the wire is joined for hanging.

3. **Tree:** Cut a length of wire that is the height you want your tree to be. Three to four inches high is about right for a tree ornament, depending on the buttons. Twist one end of the wire to hold the bottom buttons in place, and slide several brown buttons on the bottom for the tree trunk. These can be smaller buttons. Start stringing assorted green buttons on top of the brown buttons to make the graduated shape of the tree, larger buttons at the bottom and smaller buttons as you move up. If you can find a star button to add on the top, that would be a nice finishing touch! If you don't have a star button, two gold star stickers can be stuck together and fastened at the top. Twist the end of the wire into a loop so the buttons don't fall off. Tie a piece of ribbon at the top for hanging on the Christmas tree.

52 Weeks of Service Cards

Jesus came to serve God and others, and he calls us to serve just as he did. Use a deck of playing cards to create a year's worth of service ideas for your family.

Materials needed: One deck of playing cards, plain index cards, glue, yearly calendar, permanent felt-tip marker

Time required: 30 minutes

1. Count to make sure your deck of cards includes 52 cards, one card for each week of the year.

2. Cut the index cards to the exact size of the playing cards, and glue one white index card over the numbered side of the playing cards.

3. Take out the yearly calendar and note important dates on it, such as Christmas, birthdays, Easter, vacations, and other events your family celebrates.

4. Spend time together brainstorming a list of ways you could serve God and other people throughout the year (for example, collecting food for the local food bank, helping an elderly neighbor rake leaves, volunteering to serve a meal at a local mission or homeless shelter, collecting blankets for people who are homeless). Really take the time to talk about things your family could do together.

5. Write one service idea on each playing card. It's okay to write down some ideas more than once, such as collecting food to deliver to the food bank, because these kinds of blessings are needed many times throughout the year.

6. When you have your deck of cards ready, shuffle the deck and keep it in a place where you get together for family time each week. Draw one idea per week, and enjoy serving God and others together.